. . . L

Connecting with Your Husband

...LIFELINES...

CONNECTING
WITH YOUR
HUSBAND

GARY SMALLEY

Tyndale House Publishers, Inc.
WHEATON, ILLINOIS

Visit Tyndale's exciting Web site at www.tyndale.com

Designed by Ron Kaufmann

Published in association with the literary agency of Alive Communications, Inc., 7680 Goddard Street, Suite 200, Colorado Springs, CO 80920

Library of Congress Cataloging-in-Publication Data

Smalley, Gary.
    Connecting with your husband / Gary Smalley.
        p. cm. — (Life lines)
Includes bibliographical references.
    ISBN 0-8423-6019-0 (pbk.)
    1. Wives—Religious life. 2. Husbands—Psychology. 3. Marriage—Religious aspects—Christianity. 4. Man-woman relationships—Religious aspects—Christianity. I. Title. II. Series.
BV4528.15 .S64 2003
248.8′435—dc21   2002152208

Printed in the United States of America

07 06 05 04
7   6   5   4   3

The Life Lines series is designed for *real* people in *real life* situations. Written by published authors who are experts in their field, each book covers a different topic and includes:

- information you need, in a quick and easy-to-read format
- practical advice and encouragement from someone who's been there
- "life support"—hands-on tips to give you immediate help for the problems you're facing
- "healthy habits"—long-term strategies that will enrich your life
- inspiring Bible verses
- lists of additional resources—books, Web sites, videos, and seminars to keep you headed on the right path

Life Lines is a joint effort from Marriage Alive International and Smalley Relationship Center. Marriage Alive founders and directors David and Claudia Arp serve as general editors.

Whether you need assistance for an everyday situation, a life transition, or a crisis period, or you're just looking for a friend to come alongside you, Life Lines offers wise, compassionate counsel from someone who can help. This series will connect with you, inspire you, and give you tools that will change your life—for the better!

Titles in the series:
Life Lines: Connecting with Your Husband—Gary Smalley
Life Lines: Connecting with Your Wife—Barbara Rosberg

. . . CONTENTS . . .

. . . ACKNOWLEDGMENTS . . .

I want to thank Karen Kingsbury, who helped me write this book. Karen is my favorite fiction author. In fact, Karen and I teamed up for a fiction series—the Redemption series—which debuted in 2002. I couldn't have written this book without her help, and I thank God that she has agreed to work with me again in the future.

I'd also like to thank Greg Johnson, my agent, not only for having the creative ability to put together contracts that will glorify God but also for shepherding me through what feels like a second publishing life.

And a loving thanks to my wife and forever love, Norma, for standing by me through the years and for taking the time to truly understand me. Also to our children and family, and the folks at the Smalley Relationship Center for their constant support and encouragement.

D*o you ever wonder* . . .

- why your husband gives one-word answers to your questions?
- why when you vent about a frustrating coworker or a clueless salesperson, he launches into point-by-point instructions on how you could address the situation next time?
- why he cringes every time you say the word *emotions*?
- how he can come home after a stressful day, walk in the door to shrieking kids and a stopped-up sink, and immediately be ready for sex?
- why it takes him five hours after losing a game of Monopoly to talk to you again?
- why he can remember the batting average of every player on his favorite baseball team but can't remember to rinse the sink after he brushes his teeth or pick up the kids after soccer practice?

If you've ever been stymied by your husband's behavior or convinced that he's speaking a completely different language, then this book is for you! Make yourself comfortable, and let's delve into a topic that's a mystery for many women: the inner workings of a man. The information here will help you understand the man in your life—a man you love and are committed to, but who sometimes drives you crazy.

How do I know this book will help? Because I've spent hundreds of hours counseling couples whose main problems stemmed from the fact that they didn't understand each other.

My guess is you've picked up this book because you'd like to figure out your husband. Someone who sometimes seems about as foreign to you as leaving the toilet seat up. Someone with habits and vocabulary and personality traits that can make you laugh out loud—or cry yourself to sleep.

Misunderstandings between you and your husband keep your marriage from being the best it can be. They can bring frustration and resentment and, in some cases, can even lead to constant arguing, depression, and broken relationships.

I'm sure that's not what you want for your marriage—and it's also not what God wants. The first mention of marriage in the Bible refers to the permanent and intimate relationship God planned for couples: "For this reason a man will leave his father and mother and be united to his wife, and they will become one flesh" (Genesis 2:24 NIV). Marriage is a gift from God. It's an opportunity for two people to support, encourage, and sustain each other as long as they both shall live. But how do you reach that goal of one-flesh unity if you're frustrated and distracted by things your husband says or does that you just don't understand?

This book will help you get a grasp on the differences between husbands and wives and the problems that arise as a result of those differences. You'll receive the very latest research on the distinctions between men and women. After surveying and counseling thousands of people and researching the

> **Misunderstandings between you and your husband keep your marriage from being the best it can be.**

scientific reasons for the differences between men and women, I've come up with some information that might open your eyes and let you see men like you've never seen them before.

As you learn about these differences, I am confident that you will better understand your husband. You'll understand the way he talks and the way he acts related to the specific areas of communication, intimacy, competition, and daily living.

I'll give you Life Support advice that's easy to implement and will help you ease the day-to-day friction that might exist between you and the man you love.

Then you'll be given tools to enable you to establish some Healthy Habits. Tools that will help you express your love for your husband in a way that will work for both of you. Habits that will help you "cleave" to him and will give you a smoother road for your relationship all through this journey of life.

My hope is that you'll keep my name out of it (us guys have to stick together) but pass on the information to your friends. Because the truth is, guys have a lot of shortcomings when it comes to relationships. And most women I've met need a great deal of help understanding the man in their life—a man they love with all their being but sometimes can't relate to any better than, say, a bologna sandwich.

Ready? Okay, here's the lowdown on us guys.

MEN: THE MORE TROUBLING SEX

The joke goes like this: A man was walking along the road one day when a genie stopped him and offered him a single wish.

"Well," the man said, scratching his chin. "I've always wanted a bridge to Hawaii."

"A bridge to Hawaii?" The genie's jaw went slack.

"I hate flying," the man explained. "But I love the islands. Imagine how often I could travel to Hawaii if there was a bridge from here to there."

The genie began to sweat. "Have you considered how much steel is involved in something like that? What kinds of supports that type of bridge would need to sustain the force of the Pacific?" The genie

> *Be humble and gentle. Be patient with each other, making allowance for each other's faults because of your love. Always keep yourselves united in the Holy Spirit, and bind yourselves together with peace.*
>
> EPHESIANS 4:2-3

drew a deep breath. "Isn't there something else you'd rather have?"

The man pursed his lips and gazed into the sky. Then his eyes widened. "Actually, there is. I've always struggled with understanding women. I had trouble getting along with my sisters, my mother, and now my wife. If I could have one wish, it would be that I might really and truly understand women."

The genie blinked twice. "You want that bridge two lanes or four?"

That's the joke.

But the more I hear from women, the more I realize the truth is no laughing matter. At least from your vantage point.

In reality, we men are wired so differently that *we're* the ones who need to be understood. You, after all, are born so attuned to personal interaction that you almost have a built-in relationship manual. Men, well, we're a different species altogether, and you need to know why—especially if harmony with the man you love is what you desire.

Want to know why your husband is hard to talk to and sometimes insensitive, dominating, or driven? Curious about why he doesn't seem interested in your hobbies or friendships, why he doesn't respond to your desire to know about his day?

Keep reading. The secrets are just ahead.

Because of the limited space in this book, we'll need to generalize. Not every man will exhibit the characteristics I'll talk about—or perhaps not to the extreme I'll talk about—but a great many will.

WOMEN ARE FROM THE CLASSROOM; MEN ARE FROM THE PLAYGROUND

One of the simplest ways to note the differences between men and women is to watch them with their children. If you've ever left the children with Dad or watched your brother handle his children, you know what I'm talking about.

It isn't that men aren't loving and concerned; we are. Truly. It's just that the chemical differences in our brains mean we handle children in a fatherly, not motherly, fashion. Keep in mind that we're talking generalities here, but they are generalities that apply to the majority of guys.

A mom's day with the kids includes:
- neatly laid out clothing
- matching socks
- clean underwear
- clean hands and faces

- structured, timed activities all within predetermined safety standards
- planned meals pulling foods from all major food groups, including carrots and broccoli
- specific bedtimes
- chores and predetermined rules about running in the house and jumping on furniture
- a standard cleanup time that involves all children

A dad's day with the kids includes:
- mismatched clothes
- mismatched socks
- dirty clothes
- dirty hands and faces
- questionable, sometimes dangerous activities
- questionable food, including Twinkies, soda pop, and candy necklaces, moments before dinner
- loose bedtimes
- loose house rules
- few cleanup guidelines

Or, as Bill Cosby once said while imitating his children's reaction to a day alone with him, "Dad is great! Gives us that chocolate cake!"

Granted, the children love the idea of spending a day with Dad. The above activities make for a day filled with laughter and fond memories . . . and one that will require two days of follow-up once Mom's back in the picture. One man I counseled put it this way:

"When my wife's gone and I'm alone with the kids, I like to have fun and play hard. I never understand why she's upset when she gets home. The kids are safe; we've had a good time. What's the problem?"

The problem is, when analyzed through the eyes of a woman, the actions of a man can seem careless, potentially dangerous, or almost childish. Would it amaze you to know that the man you love—this unique creation of God, whom you are trying to understand—might have a reason for the way he acts? Could there be a scientific basis for why he responds the way he does? Why he says the things he says? We'll get to

---

TEN MALE CHARACTERISTICS

Eighty percent of men exhibit these strongly male characteristics:

- Aggressive behavior
- Factual
- Less emotional or unemotional
- Not talkative
- Powerful
- Great desire to win
- Strong need to conquer
- Driven personality
- Not very sensitive emotionally
- Not very sensitive to physical touch

Nearly all these personality traits stem from the first characteristic: aggressive behavior.

. . .

that in just a minute. But first let's take a brief glimpse at the man's man hall of fame.

Scripps-Howard News Service, 1992—A Colorado man drove out of a gas station near Washington, Pennsylvania, and continued on through West Virginia and part of Ohio without realizing that his wife—the mother of their two children—was still back at the gas station in Pennsylvania. In Ohio, the man pulled over and—assuming everything was well in the back of the van—decided to take a nap. It was only ninety minutes later that he awoke and recognized the fact that his wife was no longer in the vehicle. At this point he turned around and began driving frantically back east on Route 70 getting as far as Wheeling, West Virginia, where he hit a deer. The crash damaged the van, so he hoofed it to a truck stop where a trucker helped reunite him with his wife.

This happened on Mother's Day.

Okay, so you believe me already. You could write stories of your own about strange situations or odd

---

**THE GOAL: LEARNING TO UNDERSTAND
THE MAN IN YOUR LIFE**

- Learn to talk to him
- Learn to share with him
- Learn to play with him
- Learn to live with him

behaviors exhibited by the man you love. The question is this: *Why are men so different?* And the answer is simple: testosterone.

THE BIG "T"

Evidence today suggests that physiology may shape a man's personality and tendencies. What that means is *testosterone.*

A miraculous physiological occurrence happens to an unborn baby between the fifth and seventh week of development, and the outcome makes a vast difference in the male or female tendencies of that person. Baby-girl brains are very much like baby-boy brains until this point in fetal development. But this is what happens: Between the fifth and seventh week something like a faucet turns on inside both the masculine and feminine brain and drips microscopic amounts of testosterone onto the baby's brain. Whereas the girls get a few drops here and there, the boys' brains are fairly soaked in the stuff.

> A miraculous physiological occurrence happens to an unborn baby between the fifth and seventh week of development, and the outcome makes a vast difference in the male or female tendencies of that person.

We will refer to this male hormone as big T.

Testosterone makes people aggressive; there's no way around this scientific truth. The principle even holds among animals and has been proven in multiple experiments. When researchers inject monkeys with big T, the monkeys become so aggressive that they very nearly overpower their fellow monkeys. The female canary, which no longer sings once it has become an adult, will sing once more when injected with testosterone.

One study referenced in the book *Brain Sex* by Anne Moir and David Jessel showed that because of testosterone men are 50 percent more aggressive than the average female.[1] In addition, men are five times more likely than women to commit murder and twenty times more likely than women to commit a robbery.[2]

Male and female characteristics

The amount of big T that drips on the brain during fetal development will determine how strongly a child demonstrates certain characteristics typically considered male or female.

A brain soaked in testosterone is . . .

- assertive
- individualistic
- self-confident
- self-reliant
- competitive
- rough

- playful
- singly focused

A brain not soaked in testosterone is . . .

- nurturing
- considerate
- affectionate
- gentle
- compassionate for those in pain
- multiple-task minded
- emotional
- generous[3]

The amount of big T that washes over an unborn baby's brain is going to determine—at least in part—his or her personality as an adult. And there are a host of real-life situations that are affected by the fact that a man, in general, has more testosterone permeating his brain than a woman has.

What are some of the affected areas? We'll examine four: communication, intimacy, recreation, and daily routine. To begin with, let's take a look at the way men and women communicate.

> **The amount of big T that washes over an unborn baby's brain is going to determine—at least in part—his or her personality as an adult.**

COMMUNICATION: WHAT'S HE REALLY SAYING?

Now that you understand the chemical reason why boys generally have stronger, more aggressive personalities than girls, let's look at the way that personality shows itself in children—and their conversations. One study by Harvard's Preschool Program placed a small microphone on the shirts or dresses of a group of children ages two to four. A tape recorder caught every sound they made for an extended period of time, and the results will probably not surprise those of you struggling to understand your husband.

According to the study, a whopping 100 percent of the noises made by the little girls were made for the purpose of communication. In other words, they used real words to convey real thoughts or questions to themselves or other children.

However, only 68 percent of the boys' noises were made with the intention of communicating. The other 32 percent of their sounds were, well, just sounds.[4] Here's a sampling of what the researchers heard on their tapes:

Girl noises

- "Hi, Susie."
- "How are you?"
- "I got a new outfit."
- "I'm happy today."
- "Where is the teacher?"
- "What are we doing with the crayons?"
- "I like your lunch box."
- "Wanna play with me?"
- "Wanna talk?"

Boy noises

- "Rerrerrerrerrerrer . . ."
  (The sound of a truck)
- "Shhhhhhhhhhhhhhhhoooo . . ."
  (The sound of an airplane)
- "Swishhhhhhh . . . Swishhhhhhhh . . ."
  (The sound of a sword)

- "Pkew, pkew pkew . . . tatatatata . . ."
  (The sound of a gun)
- "Rurrrrrrrrrrrrr . . . Rurrrrrrrrrrrrrr . . ."
  (The sound of a siren)
- "Ruf, ruf . . . Ooooohoooohooooooo . . ."
  (The sounds of animals)
- "Ughhhhhhhhhh!" (Screaming sounds)
- "Ahhhhhhhh . . . ha ha ha ha" (Laughing, shouting sounds)

Now, we guys would tell you that those sounds actually *are* communication. But they communicate a statement such as, "I'm the biggest truck, so get out of my way."

I've found that this same phenomenon—vastly different means of communication—exists in adult men and women everywhere I go.

HE WON'T TALK

You probably know what I mean. When you see your husband at the end of the day, you say, "Hi, honey! How was your day?"

"Fine." The word sounds like the grown-up version of a truck noise.

You trail after him into the kitchen. "How was your meeting?" you ask. After spending the day apart, you're hoping for a lengthy, detailed answer—and hoping he'll ask some questions of his own.

. . .

Instead, he opens the refrigerator, pulls out a can of pop, and says, "Fine." If you listen carefully, you'll hear what is really an adult airplane sound.

In many houses the conversation goes on this way until the man finishes dinner, makes several more noises, and then plops down in front of the television. Here he releases a comfortable sigh that an hour later will be replaced with snoring.

Sounds. I'm not revealing any real secrets when I say we're also known for loud body noises. Just great big little boys romping about in the play yard of life.

Men are not big on detail

The same lack of real words and dialogue is true when men and women talk about their appearance. Take something as simple as a haircut. Two women meet, and one notices a change in the other's hairstyle.

"Wow, Janice, did you get your hair cut?"

"Yes, I went to Le Classy Styles!" She does a slight twirl and waves her fingers dramatically at her hair.

Studying each tendril of Janice's hair as though searching for a lost set of car keys, Janice's friend sucks in a deep breath. "It's absolutely to die for!"

Janice wrinkles her nose. "You're sure it doesn't make my neck look too long?"

. . .

"Too long?" Her friend gasps. "Definitely not. You look like a model. Just the way it curls under and the extra shine. What shampoo did she use?"

"It was a salon mix. The woman said this style would even help my shoulders look slimmer."

"Definitely. No doubt about it." Janice's friend frowns. "What's the phone number for the shop? I need something new, too. My hair's been looking mousy, and it's just about time I made a change. . . ."

It could go on that way for an hour and neither woman, not once, would get bored with the topic of Janice's new hairdo.

Take a man in the same situation. If he notices that his friend got a haircut, he might (we're not talking major odds here) say something like, "Hey, you got your hair cut."

To which his friend will probably say something profound like, "Yep."

And the conversation will be over.

As a wife, you probably want meaningful communication, memorable conversations, and friendly chit-chat—and instead you get little more than you did decades earlier as a little girl on the playground. This is because a man's brain operates so very differently from yours. And it's this very truth that often makes it difficult to establish and maintain the close, communicative relationship you so desire.

The search for measurable data

One of the passages of text I've found that comes close to describing the way men act in most relationships is this one from the book *Dave Barry's Complete Guide to Guys*:

> "How could he?" [a woman] will ask her best friends. "What was he thinking?"
>
> The answer is, he wasn't thinking in the sense that women mean the word. He can't. He doesn't have the appropriate type of brain. He has a guy brain, which is basically an analytical, problem-solving type of organ. It likes things to be definite and measurable and specific. It's not comfortable with nebulous and imprecise relationship-type concepts such as love and need and trust. If the guy brain has to form an opinion about another person, it prefers to form that opinion based on something concrete about the person, such as his or her earned-run average.[5]

Some of the couples I've interviewed would agree wholeheartedly with this description. If they had captured some of their early conversations they might have sounded something like this couple:

Paul and Pam met each other three months ago and

decided to start dating. Now they're sitting at a small café sipping a latte when Pam sighs contentedly. "Did you know it's our anniversary, Paul? We've been together three months. Isn't that something?"

What Pam really means is that she's wondering where the relationship is headed. Is it serious? Is it forever? Do they share the types of goals and dreams and beliefs to make a marriage work?

But Paul takes a swig of his coffee and stares at his empty dessert plate. *Three months?* he thinks to himself. *That means my jeep needs an oil change. Yes, I'm sure I haven't had it in since before Pam and I met.* . . . So he says, "Wow, I didn't realize it had been that long."

Across the table Pam blinks and measures each syllable of Paul's response carefully in her heart, mind, and soul. Of all the things she hoped he might say, his actual answer was certainly not one of them. *I get it,* she thinks to herself. *He's feeling like three months is too long, like he's trapped and I'm trying to stifle his freedom. Well, maybe I need freedom too.*

She lifts her chin, doing her best to save face. "So you're saying three months is too long, is that it?"

Paul sets his coffee cup down and swallows hard. There's something faint in Pam's tone that makes him slightly concerned that the conversation has ventured into uncharted territory. "No . . . ," he offers.

But when her expression remains unchanged he clears his throat. "Actually, yes. I . . . I didn't know it had been so long."

Pam can't believe this is happening. Paul was supposed to be the man of her dreams, the one God had chosen for her alone. Now he's waffling over whether their three months together has seemed like an unbearable six months. *Or maybe it's gone by faster because I'm not that important to him,* she reasons. Tears form in her eyes. "What exactly are you trying to say?"

He shrugs and gives her a hesitant smile. "I need my oil changed."

And in this manner we often find ourselves in debates and arguments and ruined relationships—all because the guy brain and the girl brain are so completely different.

On top of that, the human brain keeps something of a word count. Here's a fact that won't surprise you if you've spent any amount of time trying to get your husband to talk: A man's word count is less than half that of a woman.

HE HAS A LIMITED WORD COUNT

Studies show that the average male uses about 12,000 words a day, the entire day, and most of those are spent relating to people while on the job. Remember, most men are aggressive and driven. They will talk at length in the workplace in order to successfully complete an assignment, project, or task.

A woman, on the other hand, averages 25,000 words per day. Now these aren't just any words but words that must connect with people or emotions. In other words, when a woman spends her day in the workplace, generally there are few opportunities for her to really dig in and use her allotment of words.

Here's the problem. At the end of the day—whether the woman works in an office or in the home—there is a huge difference between the man's word count and the woman's. A man has spent nearly all his words. He comes home tired and drained, looking

---

HOW A MAN MIGHT SPEND HIS DAILY WORD COUNT:

- Giving instructions to other employees
- Giving his input to coworkers
- Debating the current challenges of his job with coworkers at lunchtime
- Talking to customers
- Talking to his boss
- Giving input at business meetings
- Making business phone calls

HOW A WOMAN MIGHT SPEND HER DAILY WORD COUNT:

- Lengthy conversations with other women
- Phone calls to friends, sometimes to describe the details of one single event
- Storytelling to children
- Recapping stories she has read or heard on television
- Sharing thoughts with a friend or sister

---

for a place to recharge for the next day's battle at the office.

A woman, however, is just warming up. She has thousands of words left to speak, and since her husband's word count is depleted, the conversations often wind up sounding like nothing more than question-and-answer sessions.

HIS CONVERSATIONS ARE
NOT COMMUNICATION

The following example shows how a woman might use her word count when she's reunited with her husband at day's end. At the same time, it demonstrates how the man conserves his words.

The daily question-and-answer session

The woman begins with a seemingly simple question. "How are you?"

The man, occasionally even making eye contact, will utter, "Fine."

The woman tries again. "How was work?"

"Good."

And suddenly the ball is rolling in a way the man feels helpless to stop, knowing with utmost certainty that when it stops he'll somehow be underneath.

The woman sighs. "Anything interesting or out of the usual happen?"

. . .

"Nope."

"Any interesting conversations with anyone?"

"No."

"Did you get that project finished, the one you were working on yesterday?"

"Yes."

"How did it go?"

"Great."

"Did the presentation work out like you thought it would?"

"Yes."

"You seem a little tired; did anything bad happen?"

"No."

"But you're not excited. I mean, I thought you'd be happy to see me. I've been looking forward to talking to you all day and now it doesn't seem like you have anything to say. Are you upset with me about something?"

"No, not at all."

"So you had a good day?"

"Yes."

"Well, guess what?"

"What?"

"Timmy came home from school early because that mean child, Joey, kicked him in the chin again. Only this time it was because Timmy was brave enough to defend a little girl—a girl Joey was picking on."

"Mm-hmm."

"Are you listening to me?"

"Yes."

"Because the truth is, I think Timmy has a very tender heart, which means he might get picked on in junior high. And even though he's only in third grade, junior high is just around the corner, don't you think?"

"Sure."

"So does it worry you?"

"What?"

"Timmy! And his tender heart! I think he's a lot like me, honey, and you know I have a very soft heart. So what I'm saying is maybe you should spend a little more time with him, you know, man-to-man, to help him figure out how to handle the boys who are so mean at school. Then maybe he won't have any trouble when he gets in junior high. Would that be okay?"

Pause.

"Could you spend more time with Timmy?"

"Sure."

"You know, it doesn't feel like you're really listening to me. I wait all day to talk to you and this is what I get. Just a couple of one-word answers."

Pause.

"See. You have nothing to say to me. How am I supposed to believe you love me when you can't even talk to me?"

Pause.

"Fine. I'm going to my room. You can find me there if you decide you want to talk."

"Okay."

Take a look at that dialogue and see if it doesn't come awfully close to what you're used to. It might even make you laugh out loud. It did for my wife. Why? Because even though I'm aware of my word deficiency, I still have a tendency to minimize my words once I get home at night.

> Studies show that the average male uses about 12,000 words a day, the entire day, and most of those are spent relating to people while on the job.

The woman in the above scenario is thinking, *If he really loved me, he'd talk to me.* But let me give you a secret about the man and his thought process throughout a dialogue like that one.

What the man isn't thinking
- I'm mad at her, so I won't say much tonight.
- I don't like her.
- I don't want to talk to someone like her.
- She isn't important to me.
- I don't care about what she has to say.

. . .

What the man is thinking

- I wonder how long until dinner.
- It sure is good to be home.
- I wish she'd give me a hug.
- I'm glad she's interested about my day.
- The day is finally over and now I can relax.

Are you seeing something here that could help you understand the man you love? He isn't mad at you, doesn't hate you, and isn't bored with your company. He's simply out of words. Should he learn to stretch his word count? Yes. But in this book we're dealing with understanding men, and for that reason we'll be looking at what you can do to help your husband find more to say.

Count up the words above and you'll see this ratio: The woman is out-speaking the man 342 words to 20. And though it sounds extreme, this type of conversation is common and happens in houses all over the world.

> *Kind words are like honey— sweet to the soul and healthy for the body.*
>
> PROVERBS 16:24

If this happens at your house, at this point in a conversation like the one above you'll be speaking roughly seventeen times as many words as your husband. In a few hours you'll have reached your word count, all right. But you'll be so frustrated you'll want to go to bed early and sleep with your back to the

. . .

man you love, balancing yourself on the edge of the mattress.

Your husband? He may want intimacy—physical intimacy. And he'll be baffled at why you don't feel the same way.

A MAN WANTS THE FACTS

If the conversation ever gets to the point where the woman sighs and says, "Honey, I want to talk . . . ," the first thing out of the man's mouth will almost always be, "About what?"

He wants the facts, ma'am. Nothing but the facts. As soon as you get close to running out of facts, he gets bored and uninterested. Here are some hurtful things he's likely to say if you launch into a lengthy discussion about something that doesn't involve facts:

- "What's the point?"
- "Is this going somewhere?"
- "How long is this conversation going to last?"
- "What are you trying to say?"

If it isn't a fact, the man in your life will tend not to be very interested. Yes, this is painful, and this is where the crisis areas spring from. But help is on the way.

LIFE SUPPORT: MAKING FACT OUT OF FEELINGS

Imagine that you're married to the man of your dreams, and both of you live during the days when the Tower of Babel was built. One day your husband comes home, and instead of English, he's speaking Hebrew.

There you stand, face-to-face, toe-to-toe, each of you bursting with love for the other but with no way to communicate that love.

In a sense, this is a great picture of men and women throughout the ages, with one exception: The language barrier is not sudden or new. It has always been in place.

Now if you were living during the Tower of Babel days and were desperate to find a way to communicate love and emotions and feelings and thoughts to the man you love, you'd probably be creative. You'd look for tools, you'd draw pictures, you'd speak in slow, short sentences until you were sure he was actually understanding you.

This is exactly what I'm asking you to do starting now, even minutes after you set down this book. Try communicating your feelings in a way that uses facts, objects, and object lessons—whatever it takes to trick his brain. Here are some examples:

- (Showing him an empty box) "Honey, this is how my life feels today—empty."

- (Pointing to the clean kitchen counter) "Do you know how I cleaned the counter? One item at a time. I put away everything that was cluttering this counter. That's what I want you to do with that issue at work. Take one thing at a time and tell me about it."

- (Holding up a newspaper) "There was a story in here about high school seniors going off to college. All their parents said they can't believe their children have grown up so quickly. Have you considered spending more time with Timmy?"

- (Pointing to your marked-up calendar) "We've made time for lots of things this month, but not for you and me. Let's find an open date and go out to dinner."

RULES FOR FAIR FIGHTING

Conflict is inevitable, even if you and your husband communicate well. When you do have disagreements, follow these suggestions for fighting fair:

1. Love, love, love.
2. Reveal your positions.
3. Communicate freely.
4. Remain matter-of-fact.
5. Analyze the different positions you each bring and discuss them as a couple.
6. Decide on the best decision for you as a couple.
7. Agree not to be angry or emotional.
8. Don't look back.

Adapted from *Food and Love* by Gary Smalley

HEALTHY HABIT: EXPANDING
HIS WORD COUNT

It is important to remember that though you struggle, though you barrage your husband with more questions than the woman in the example above, you will probably never succeed in getting him to talk at the level you want, every day of the week and every week of the year. This can be very troubling in the early years of marriage, especially after the dating and engagement period when talking seemed to be such an integral part of your relationship.

The truth is, the man was fact-finding, learning more about the woman he would one day marry. But after one or more years of marriage, you will probably meet at the end of the day and be very disappointed in the amount of information he's willing to share.

But there's hope. Through my seminars and counseling experiences, I have seen hundreds of couples grow in this area, usually when the woman is willing to work on expanding her husband's word count.

Ways to expand a man's word count
- Do not ask him multiple questions immediately upon seeing him at day's end.
- Don't expect lengthy conversations until he's had a chance to unwind.
- Choose your conversations carefully.

- Choose the timing and location of your conversations carefully.
- Have object lessons and factual details ready.

What do I mean by "Choose your conversations carefully"? Well, if you have a lot to say about a sale you attended earlier in the day or about a coworker's struggles with her sister-in-law, the man you love will likely tune you out. If you make these types of conversations—those that are irrelevant to your own relationship and life—a regular part of your communication with your husband, he may assume you never have anything important to say.

Remember, we're talking important by his male-brain standards. That has nothing to do with his love for you.

In your opinion every conversation, every word, every syllable is highly important and worth sharing. In fact, you're probably bursting at the seams for the chance to share these things with him.

> You will probably never succeed in getting your husband to talk at the level you want, every day of the week and every week of the year.

But this book is supposed to help you better understand a man's way of thinking. And many men won't want to hear details about anything other than you, the kids, the family, or whatever affects any of you directly.

As for the timing and location, take a look at the following situations. Some are conducive for conversations with a man, and others aren't.

Good places and times to talk to a typical man
- At the dinner table, after dinner
- On the sofa when he mutes the commercials
- On the sofa after a television program is over
- On a walk or bike ride
- In the car with the radio off
- On the porch or deck when there are no pressing deadlines
- In bed when he wants to be intimate (he may be especially open to your heart at this time)
- Just about anywhere on the weekend, when his word count is still fresh

Bad places and times to talk to a man
- Before dinner while he's reading the paper or working in the kitchen (Too much chaos.)
- During a favorite televised sports event or television program (Too distracted.)
- On the court while playing an intense tennis match or other sporting event (Too distracted.)
- In the car with the radio blaring (Too distracted.)
- Anywhere in the minutes before an approaching

deadline (Too focused on the upcoming event. This is a highly factual moment for guys.)

- In bed when you've already begun being physically intimate (Highly distracted. This could even result in hurt feelings if he feels you're not engaged in the physical part of your relationship.)
- Anywhere on busy days when he has little time between work and the next meeting, child's sports event, etc.

HEALTHY HABIT: MEN ENJOY WORD PICTURES

Oftentimes your husband intends to be very sensitive and intuitive to your wants and needs, but he is unable to grasp your situation without a word picture. One that has worked well with couples I've counseled is the "gas tank" example. It goes something like this.

You explain to your husband that your need for conversation is as important to your heart as gasoline is to a car. Once he grasps this picture—which for most men will happen instantly—you can easily say to him the following things and he'll immediately understand:

> *Your own soul is nourished when you are kind, but you destroy yourself when you are cruel.*
>
> PROVERBS 11:17

- "My tank is low."
- "I'm running on empty."

- "I need you to top off my tank."
- "I need a complete fill up."

See if using this type of word picture will help develop your man's ability to communicate. Remember, if he feels like he's accomplishing something, he'll be much more likely to participate. Filling up the tank of his one true love through communicating is something most men can understand and accomplish.

. . . 3 . . .

INTIMACY: GETTING CLOSE
TO YOUR MAN

One of my favorite books describing the differences
in intimacy between men and women is *Men Are from
Mars, Women Are from Venus* by John Gray. He truly
goes into detail about why men and women struggle
so much with this issue. For example, Gray writes that
sharing personal feelings is more important and fulfilling to most women than achieving specific goals
is. Women tend to be relationship oriented, while
men tend to be goal oriented.[6] When men face a problem, they tend to withdraw. When women face a
problem, they tend to seek out others and talk
through their concerns.[7]

Is it any wonder that we struggle? Men and women

have different ideas about what intimacy entails. Most women crave a deep connection with their husband. But in order to form that kind of connection, husbands must first share their deepest feelings—something that's extremely difficult for most men.

AN INABILITY TO FEEL

I once counseled a man who was an extreme fact finder. He wasn't able to articulate any feelings and struggled when it came to relating to his wife and children. As I counseled the man, I learned that feelings were forbidden in the home he grew up in. His father barked terse commands at him, but never—not once that this man could remember—did his father ever put an arm around his shoulders and draw him close. Never did he kiss him on the forehead or pat him on the back or say the words every child needs so desperately to hear: "I love you."

This man never thought much about the fact that his father was so emotionally closed off until one dark winter day when a policeman knocked at his door. The news was something every parent dreads. His thirteen-year-old son had been riding his bike and was hit by a drunk driver. He died at the scene.

I remember when this angry, hurting man told me that he'd gone to his son's gravesite but had been unable to cry. He told me, "I saw my wife shed tears of sorrow, and I watched the hurt expressed by many of our friends and family members. But as much as I wanted to, I couldn't release my grief with tears. I just couldn't feel it. I bottled up the pain inside and pulled back into a shell."

Then a few weeks after the funeral, he shared with me that God did something very special to open his eyes to what he was going through and what was happening in his heart.

He was out in his woodshed, working on a project, trying to take his mind off of what had happened. He'd been sanding a piece of fairly rough pine when his finger slid along the edge of the board and a long, needle-sharp splinter shoved almost an inch into his thumb. The pain was excruciating, and when he pulled out the splinter, his thumb began bleeding profusely.

> A man who can cry is a man who has learned some secrets about intimacy.

As the man stood there in the shed—tears in his eyes, his thumb throbbing—a picture began to form in his mind of a day on a lake when he was ten years old. He and his stern father were fishing, and he fell and hooked his thumb on a long barbed fishhook. His father made him pull out the fishhook. The angry man began shouting at his son for having tears in his eyes. Then he beat him in a way the man remembers to this day.

. . .

"Men do not cry," his father yelled as the beating continued.

The memory faded. At that moment—there in the woodshed behind his home, just weeks after his own son's death—the man suddenly realized he had been living under that guideline ever since. Men can't feel; it's not allowed.

"When my son died it was like a sword pierced my heart," the man told me at our counseling session. "But I couldn't show any emotion, because men don't cry; they don't show their feelings."

The man knew that he couldn't move another inch without removing the sword of grief from his heart. Yes, it would bleed, but he would never heal any other way. So then and there, overwhelmed by the picture of his past and the emotion that had been dammed up in his heart for weeks, he began to shake.

The sword was suddenly gone and tears, real tears, began to flow from his eyes.

For what felt like hours, the man stood there in his woodshed, sobbing, weeping for the boy he'd lost. It was the first time he could ever remember really crying.

> *Two people can accomplish more than twice as much as one; they get a better return for their labor. If one person falls, the other can reach out and help. But people who are alone when they fall are in real trouble. And on a cold night, two under the same blanket can gain warmth from each other. But how can one be warm alone?*
>
> ECCLESIASTES 4:9-11

But thankfully it hasn't been the last.

He told me recently, "I know now that Jesus doesn't mind my tears and he feels my pain. That day in the woodshed it was like he said to me, 'I know all about your splinters. I felt them when I was on the cross. But I love you enough to let you cry and to hug away your hurt.'"

Struggles with intimacy

A man who can cry is a man who has learned some secrets about intimacy. But sadly, for many men it takes something tragic or life-changing before they understand this truth.

Here are a few ways you can tell if the man you love has trouble with intimacy or struggles to open up:

- He's unable to discuss his feelings.
- He's determined to avoid his feelings.
- He's unable to express love, sorrow, or pain.
- He's unable or unwilling to cry.
- He's determined to make all situations into a joke.
- He's determined to lighten the mood or change the topic when emotional issues are discussed.
- He physically leaves the room when emotional issues are discussed.
- He's insensitive to the emotions of those around him.

. . .

Most men—fortunately—do not undergo such traumatic experiences as the one described above. Yet many boys emerge from adolescence with a strong sense that being strong and unfeeling is the "masculine" thing to do. When a male brain is saturated in testosterone, it doesn't take much, even from well-meaning family members, to give a boy the message that emotions and feelings are only for girls.

Here are some things your husband may have heard when growing up—things that may have shaped him into a seemingly uncaring person:

- "Don't cry unless you're hurt."
- "Tough it out."
- "Boys don't cry."
- "Only sissies get hurt feelings."
- "It's a sign of weakness to let people know you're hurting."

If you love a man who doesn't seem to be able to express his feelings, you might want to consider using word pictures to help him identify what's going on inside. A word picture uses a story or object to simultaneously activate the emotions and intellect of the hearer. As a result, he experiences your words rather than just hearing them. For some examples, see the sidebar on the next page.

It's important to realize that helping your husband

PAINTING A PICTURE WITH WORDS

If you feel like your husband doesn't really understand what you say, especially when the subject has to do with emotions, try using a word picture. Here are a few examples:

- *To express your appreciation for his love:* Your love for me is like a huge glass of iced tea on a hot summer day. It's cool and crisp, and its refreshment restores my strength and quenches the thirst of my dry, dusty soul.

- *To tell him you feel overlooked:* When we were first married, I felt like a beautiful, handcrafted, leather-bound, gold-trimmed book that had been presented to you as a gift from God. At first I was received with great enthusiasm and excitement—cherished, talked about, shared with others, and handled with care. As time has gone by, I've been put on the bookshelf to collect dust. Once in a while you remember I'm here. But if only you would take me off the shelf and open me up! If only you would see how much more I have to offer you.

- *To tell him you love him:* There have been times over the years when I've faced hailstorms that I thought would turn into tornadoes. But like the shelter of a storm cellar, I can always run to you to protect me from hardship. You're as solid as a rock, and I know you'll always be there when the storm clouds blow into my life.

- *To tell him you feel overworked:* The Super Bowl is over and the players file into the locker room. Dirty uniforms are thrown on the floor, along with dirty socks and muddy cleats. The players shower and slowly file out, leaving me behind. Not only do I have to clean up the mess, but no one even knows I'm here doing it.

from *The Language of Love* by Gary Smalley and John Trent

FOR MORE INFORMATION . . .

Two great books that go into this information in detail are *Brain Sex* by Anne Moir and David Jessel and *You Just Don't Understand* by Deborah Tannen.

. . .

learn to express his feelings will take time. You might have to use several examples or try for several days, weeks, or even months before he is able to feel and share with you what's in his heart. And until he reaches that point, he won't be able to connect with you on an emotionally intimate level.

Based on what I've learned in my many years of counseling, I've found that a woman's definition of intimacy is very different from a man's. Consider the following lists:

What women mean by intimacy
- deep emotional connection
- daily time sharing your heart
- daily time hearing the heart of the one you love
- ability to cry easily and together at emotional moments
- a sensitivity to know immediately when feelings are hurt
- understanding each other's dreams and goals
- closeness of the heart and soul

What men mean by intimacy
- deep physical connection
- foreplay
- hand-holding, hugging, kissing
- understanding each other's physical needs

- an ability to communicate physical needs
- physical time alone together
- a sensitivity to know when physical needs are present

One of the reasons men may be more focused on physical closeness is that men aren't as sensitive to physical touch as women are. In other words, it takes more physical touch to meet a man's physical needs. In the same way that a woman has twice the daily word count, a man has twice the need for physical stimulation.

The point is this: Women often feel unloved because their emotional needs aren't being met, and in the same way, men often feel ignored because their physical needs aren't being met.

I think the problem is clear at this point: Guys have trouble with true emotional intimacy. Now let's take a look at some crucial information that will help you if you and your husband are struggling in this area.

> Women often feel unloved because their emotional needs aren't being met, and in the same way, men often feel ignored because their physical needs aren't being met.

LIFE SUPPORT: DON'T PUSH INTIMACY
First and foremost, there are some things you should avoid if you want your husband to become more aware of his emotions and more willing to discuss them.

. . .

- Shouting at him to "be more sensitive." This would be similar to insisting that a dog act more like a goldfish.
- Giving him the silent treatment in hopes that he'll notice something is wrong
- Belittling him for being insensitive
- Mocking him
- Threatening him. For example, saying, "Fine, I'll just talk to Joe at work. At least he cares about my feelings."
- Burying your emotions because you believe he'll never care anyway
- Withholding sex until he becomes more sensitive

The next most important piece of advice I can give you is this: *Understand that in most cases the man you love feels the same way about you that you feel about him.* In fact, he probably loves you more than life itself. But, without training, his testosterone-soaked brain makes it extremely difficult for him to open up and share his feelings or be attentive to yours. With that in mind, remember these truths about your husband:

- He loves you.
- He wants the relationship to work.
- He doesn't want to fight.

- He wants you to be happy.
- He doesn't understand your desire to focus on feelings.
- He wants to satisfy you but doesn't always know how.

So there you have it. No matter how difficult men seem to be, no matter how much trouble they have sharing their feelings and being invested in yours, they do, in nearly every case, care about you. So the pressing question is this: *How do you train a man to be more emotionally intimate?* The information in the next section will help.

HEALTHY HABITS: TRAINING A MAN TOWARD EMOTIONAL INTIMACY

The need for intimacy goes far beyond the hurt feelings you may be feeling today. It goes beyond a man's desire to be physically close. In fact, it can affect your quality of life and, in many cases, even your life span.

Love promotes healing and health
World-famous cardiologist Dr. Dean Ornish says in his book *Love and Survival*, "Anything that promotes a sense of isolation often leads to illness and suffering. Anything that promotes a sense of love and intimacy and connection, openness, and community is very

healing."[8] As a man opens up and learns how to share feelings, he learns how to feel connected in a more intimate way, and that brings very tangible benefits. Here are some of the main points Dr. Ornish found in his research:

Possible benefits of emotional intimacy
- longer life span
- better immune system
- greater overall health
- strong sense of well-being
- less illness
- more physical strength

Of course the other side has also proven to be true. Take a look at the following possible risks of being isolated emotionally:

Possible side effects of isolation
- reduced life span
- greater susceptibility to disease
- decreased ability to heal
- greater incidence of illness
- higher likelihood of emotional problems

In a sense, the more a man becomes involved in loving relationships, the greater his chances of staying healthy and the stronger his immune system. On the other hand, the person who is isolated, insensitive, not open, lacking deep friendships and loving relationships, and not giving or receiving love is five times more likely to experience a major disease or constant nagging sicknesses.

When I'm counseling a man who has trouble with emotional intimacy, I use three tools to help him recognize his deep feelings. These tools allow a man to use his logical, factual brain to tap in to emotional, intangible feelings. They work wonders in relationships where women are feeling disconnected. You can use the following tools at home. They're a good way to start developing the type of intimacy you're longing for in your relationship.

> **The more a man becomes involved in loving relationships, the greater his chances of staying healthy and the stronger his immune system.**

Tools to tap into a man's emotions

1. **Use his personal history.** Connect his current situation with an event from his past.

    Mary was a woman whose husband struggled with intimacy. She used the personal-history tool by waiting for a relaxed time when they were alone. Then she brought up an illness her husband had suffered as a child. "Honey, remember when you were sick as a child and your parents thought you might die? Remember how afraid they were?" Her husband nodded. Mary could see in his eyes that he remembered the incident clearly. "Okay," she continued. "If you had to rate your own feelings between zero and ten, ten being very afraid, how would you compare what's happening with you at work to that experience when you were sick?" Before long, Mary's husband was talking about his feelings as though he'd discovered them for the first time.

2. **Use his job.** Connect a situation in the family with a situation your husband experienced at work.

Linda was afraid her husband had concerns about their marriage that he wasn't expressing. When I told her about the tools to get a man talking about his feelings, she saw one that would easily work in her attempts at conversation. That evening she approached her husband an hour after he'd gotten home from work and said, "Honey, remember last month when your boss laid your friend off, and you were upset because he didn't check with you first?" Linda's husband snapped to attention, immediately identifying with the situation. Linda spent a few minutes talking about the layoff and whether her husband's boss was still doing those types of things. Then she said, "Am I acting like your boss in any way? You know, not checking with you on things?"

This simple setup allowed Linda's husband to reveal many feelings he'd kept buried inside— not because he didn't want to talk to Linda, but because he didn't see any point in sharing his emotions. The result for Linda and her husband was dramatic. Months later they felt close and connected and their marriage was stronger and more fulfilling than ever.

FIVE WAYS TO ENCOURAGE YOUR HUSBAND

- Say thank you. Don't reserve gratitude for big gifts, huge home-improvement projects, or just when you feel your husband "deserves" it. Be grateful for little things too! Taking out the trash, washing your car, running errands . . . all are worthy of thanks.
- Take note of his special preferences and use that knowledge to create special surprises for him. Does he love Ben & Jerry's ice cream? Buy his favorite flavor when you know he's had a bad day. Does he enjoy getting back rubs? Massage his shoulders without his asking.
- Compliment him. When he encourages a friend or is patient with your three-year-old's endless questions, let him know you noticed and thought he did a great job.
- Ask him about his dreams—and don't shoot them down! As you listen to things he would love to do, you'll learn more about your spouse and what motivates him.
- Tell him you're glad to be married to him!

3. **Use his favorite sport.** Use a sports analogy that applies to your situation.

Noreen had been looking for a way to make her marriage better, but she needed her husband's cooperation and attention to the matter. When I suggested these tools, she got a gleam in her eye. "Sports," she said. "That'll work." Her husband's favorite team had been doing poorly for the past few years, so that weekend Noreen asked him several questions about it. "Why do you think they're playing so badly?" and "What's the coach doing to make things better?" After several minutes of talk about the team, Noreen paused. Then she said, "Honey, if our marriage was a sports team, what do you think we could do to be more successful? What could we do differently?"

> *Don't be selfish; don't live to make a good impression on others. Be humble, thinking of others as better than yourself.*
>
> PHILIPPIANS 2:3

The tool helped her husband reveal his feelings, and over the next few weeks Noreen found more sports analogies to gain her husband's interest in making their marriage a national champion of sorts. Today their marriage is a wonderful example of what can happen when you learn how to help your man express his feelings.

. . .

The relational handbook

As women, you tend to have a relationship handbook in your hearts. It's built-in. You're comfortable sharing your emotions and are sensitive to the feelings of others. Now it's up to you to develop these healthy habits and, in doing so, train your husband both to express his emotions and be in tune to yours.

Here are some steps you can take to help the man you love toward a healthier life—physically, relationally, and emotionally.

- Understand that the process takes time.
- Look for moments when your husband might be most aware of his feelings:
    a friend's wedding
    a reunion
    after an emotional movie, song, or book
    a funeral
    a church service
    a long walk
    a leisurely dinner or meal alone together
- If this is a moment when he is not preoccupied, ask one or two questions, such as:
    What are you thinking?
    What do you remember about being a kid, in high school, our early days, etc.?

> If you could change anything about your life, what would you change?
>
> Tell me about your dad, brother, sister, mom, or another family member.
>
> What are your three favorite things about us?

- Realize that he may still answer these questions with one or two words.
- When he does respond by sharing his thoughts and emotions, take the time to share a few of yours.
- Incorporate this type of sharing into fun activities such as:
  - dining out
  - walking
  - driving with the radio off
  - recreational activities such as bowling, hiking, doing a puzzle, etc.

Work with the man you love and keep in mind that his brain simply isn't rigged for this type of conversation or attention to emotions. But over time and with practice, you'll make progress—especially if you are patient and make emotional talks fun. And remember, you'll both benefit from the process.

. . . 4 . . .

RECREATION: GUYS JUST
WANNA WIN

Men are competitive. They want to win even when all that's at stake is the family Scrabble title. They want to notch a victory or find a solution or invent something. They want to blaze a trail or initiate a new project. It's part of the conqueror mentality that—like it or not—goes along with being a guy.

MEN WANT TO WIN AT ALL COSTS

Testosterone levels vary in all men. A brain with anything above 300 is considered fairly saturated in testosterone. Believe it or not, levels can go higher than 1,000. Let me give you some examples of a man's

TASK	300 T LEVEL	500 T LEVEL	1,000 T LEVEL
Sports	Winning makes it fun	Winning is crucial	He can't carry on a conversation for five hours after losing
Chores	Take-charge attitude	Organize and conquer	Attack like a warrior
Work	Driven to excel	Being the best matters	No rest until he takes over the company

desire to win based on where he falls on the testosterone chart.

A man can actually have his blood or saliva tested to see how high his testosterone level is. But my guess is, his results wouldn't surprise you. After all, you're the one who spends hours of your week trying to understand him.

When it comes to recreational or work-related activities, the higher a man's testosterone level, the more competitive and solution-oriented he tends to be.

I once counseled a pastor and his wife whose congregation was actually dwindling because of the pastor's desire to win.

The congregation was fairly small—three hundred people—and the families loved to get together for church picnics and recreational nights. The problem was that no matter what the activity, the pastor had to be better than the other men. If they were playing basketball, he delivered as many cheap shots as he needed to get the rebound or basket. If they were playing touch football, he'd shamelessly beat out a ten-year-old for the ball and run it into the end zone. If they were having a watermelon-eating contest, he'd rather get sick than let someone else walk away with the title. Even if they were hiking—I'm talking about a leisurely recreational hike, not a race—this pastor would forego conversation and group walking to power his way to the end point and feel as though he had somehow "won" the hike.

"What hurts is that his attitude is carrying over into our relationship," the pastor's wife told me. "I know for sure that four families have left because the men felt bugged by my husband's attitude. And now I'm hoping I won't be next."

After weeks of discussion with this young pastor, we determined that the only way to fix the problem was for him to remove himself from the recreational activities of his church. Instead, he took on a leadership role, making the rounds at social events and overseeing the activities as they unfolded.

In the process, he took up hunting and club basketball as a way of venting his competitive nature outside the realm of the church.

This may seem extreme, but it's not out of the ordinary for many men. A man's overzealous desire to win may affect all of his relationships—from family and friends to coworkers and neighbors.

A man who tends toward an extreme attitude of winning or conquering may be willing to crush people—emotionally or physically—who stand between him and his victory, trophy, or goal. Regardless of what activity comes along, this type of man will have a single-minded, focused determination to win.

This single-mindedness can reap great results—just think of all the inventions and explorations that most likely were aided by testosterone. Unfortunately, this determination can be turned to negative things as well. Studies have shown that violent criminals have a higher testosterone level than average. The Bible is also full of examples of testosterone-charged folks trying to win at something—such as men building the Tower of Babel, Samson setting fire to his enemies' crops, or Peter slashing off the ear of a Roman soldier.

Bagging a pair of trophy shoes

When it comes to shopping, men generally see the outing as a time to conquer. Women, on the other hand, often see it as a relaxing time to chat and catch up on the week's news or browse shop after shop to see what fashions are in style.

"I'm going shopping," a woman will say. "Wanna come?"

The man thinks about that for a moment. "What for?"

"I need a pair of shoes." The woman smiles and reaches for her husband's hand. She's thinking, *This will be wonderful. Just the two of us, strolling through the mall, spending time alone together, walking hand in hand. We'll laugh and catch up on things and maybe stop for a cup of coffee before we go home.*

And he's thinking, *We'll get a pair of shoes and be home in time to watch the game.* "Okay," he says. "Let's go."

Fifteen minutes later they arrive at the mall, and he finds a front-row parking spot, which is the first step toward conquering the shoes. As they walk toward the mall entrance the woman takes the man's hand. "This'll be fun," she says, smiling.

The higher a man's testosterone level, the more competitive and solution-oriented he tends to be.

He nods, distracted, and leads her inside, where he says, "Where's the shoe store?"

She looks hard at him as though he's speaking Latin or Greek. "We don't have to go there first, do we?"

And the man is thinking, *Did I miss something? I thought we were looking for shoes.* "What else do you need?"

His words are like thumbtacks poking holes in her heart and casting a shadow of frustration on the date she'd imagined at the mall. "Well," she says, "I wanted to look around. I need a gift for a baby shower next week and then there's your mother's birthday and—"

"You didn't say anything about that." He is doing his best to keep an even tone, but at this point he can sense he's losing the battle. He draws a steadying breath. "You said shoes. You were looking for shoes."

If the tears aren't already in her eyes at this point, they're definitely forming somewhere in the near vicinity. "Fine. Let's go."

They start walking, only this time her arms are crossed. Her steps are quick and irritated. In very little time they arrive at a shoe store. She's thinking, *Fine. If he doesn't want to look around, at least I can take my time picking out a pair of shoes.*

They walk inside and he watches her slowly make the rounds along the inside perimeter of the shoe display. Irritated that she isn't finding anything, he comes alongside her. "Honey, what are you looking for?"

"Well, something comfortable. . . ." She's thinking,

> *Since God chose you to be the holy people whom he loves, you must clothe yourselves with tenderhearted mercy, kindness, humility, gentleness, and patience. You must make allowance for each other's faults and forgive the person who offends you. Remember, the Lord forgave you, so you must forgive others.*
>
> COLOSSIANS 3:12-13

. . .

If he's in that kind of hurry, how much does he really enjoy being with me? If he really loved me, he'd want to walk slowly through the mall, holding hands and talking about whatever comes to mind.

And he's thinking, *What would she do without me?* "Okay, honey, let's narrow it down. . . . Comfortable meaning what exactly?"

When the search turns up nothing, the man is not daunted. He's gone hunting before and knows that it often takes more than one effort to bag the prize catch. The same is probably true with shoes. Besides, as long as they find something in the next forty minutes he'll still make it home in time for the game.

Three stores later it has become a contest, a challenge with the ultimate prize: a pair of shoes. The exact pair of shoes, wherever they may be. He's thinking, *Whether we get home before the game starts or not, we will find these shoes.* That's his winning mentality. Anything short of driving home with a pair of shoes would leave him with the same-sized pit in his stomach he got as a high school boy when his team missed the state basketball playoffs by a single basket.

To come this close, to be surrounded by shoes and miss the one pair that his wife needs and desires is not even conceivable. So he urges her on to the next and last shoe store.

. . .

There it finally happens. The woman finds a pair of shoes and decides they're the ones for her. She's thinking, *I'm glad it took a while longer. This has been nice after all, spending extra time together and having him help me find the shoes I want. How sweet is that, anyway?*

His thoughts are focused on the yellow tag attached to the shoes. They're on sale! That's like hitting a prize buck with a towering rack of horns. It's like catching the biggest fish of the day.

Walking out of the mall minutes later, the man will almost always offer to carry the bag. Why? Because he is feeling very victorious. His heart is beating hard with thoughts of, *We did it! We bagged our trophy shoes!*

Why women don't generally hunt

This same mentality in reverse is why most hunters are men. You probably think men hunt to help cut back on the meat bill, right? Wrong. Sure, a man enjoys bringing home a month's worth of dinners and providing for his family. But he could do that at the supermarket just as successfully.

Hunting fills his recreational need to win. Women, though, are more likely to get emotionally involved on a hunting trip. A woman will spot a herd of deer while out hunting with her husband, and she'll see

Bambi, Bambi's mother, Bambi's friends and family members, Bambi's young, sweet girlfriend.

She sees relationships and interaction and strong bonds between the deer.

A man sees a trophy catch. He pictures the deer strapped to his truck and he thinks, *I'm one shot away from victory.*

I've actually heard couples tell the story of being in a deer stand together when the woman jumps up and screams out a warning to the deer: "Run! He's going to shoot!"

The husbands were absolutely furious. They didn't understand that their wives were seeing a dead father, a dead son, destroyed relationships.

This is why a woman must understand all of what drives a man. Because his brain works on a factual basis, the man in this situation is completely unable to feel emotional pain for the deer. He wants to kill the deer and mount the head on his wall. Then he'll say, "Me hunter, me did that." It's very difficult for the average woman to think that way.

LIFE SUPPORT: DON'T TAKE IT PERSONALLY

The first thing you must understand when it comes to a man's desire to win or conquer is that it's not personal. No matter how your husband acts or what he says that irritates you or makes you think he's

. . .

insensitive, the truth is he means nothing against you by his intensely driven nature.

It's very important for a woman to understand this. In fact, when a man steps back and looks at how his overanxious efforts at winning sometimes ruin relationships with people he loves, he's usually surprised. He often has no idea how his actions are being perceived.

Whenever possible, try to avoid reaching the following conclusions when your husband's desire to win gets the better of him:

- "He cares more about winning than being with me."
- "He's driven to do things that are unimportant, but he has no desire to work on our relationship."
- "He doesn't care about anyone but himself."
- "He acts like a child when he doesn't get what he wants."
- "He's too busy making things happen to care about me."

Please believe me when I tell you that most guys would be shocked to know you felt that way—even if you've told them so in those exact words. Guys are doing what comes naturally by way of their very different, very testosterone-soaked brains. They will conquer, fact-find, investigate, and blow by nearly anything that comes between them and the goal at hand, whether it's washing a car or writing a business report or playing pick-up basketball down at the health club.

Granted, a man sometimes needs to quench this thirst to conquer. He needs to choose consciously to be careful of people in his way. I hope when you read the next section you'll develop enough healthy habits to help him do so.

HEALTHY HABITS: MAKE HIM FEEL LIKE A WINNER

There's probably nothing you can do that's more powerful for your husband than starting a list of all the things you feel he's a winner at. As you compliment him in those areas, as you build him up, he will have much less need to conquer or be victorious in other aspects of life. In a sense, he will be able to relax a little.

And it's only when he's relaxed that he will have the desire and energy to talk about emotional issues or spend one-on-one time together with you.

Think about it. What praiseworthy character qualities does your husband have? Where is he ahead of the pack with his decisions, his work habits, his fathering skills, his ability as a husband? Write down

· · ·

anything and everything good you can find about him. Write little notes from time to time or cards telling him what a winner he is.

Here are some sample areas where your man might already be succeeding—areas that, if built up, will free him from the desire to win and conquer. That desire will already have been met by your words of praise.

- He helps around the house.
- He is faithful.
- He is funny.
- He is loyal.
- He is dependable with his work or with providing for the family.
- He is dependable with his children.
- He is kind.
- He is strong and can handle household tasks that require strength.
- He is confident.
- Physically, he is a good lover.
- He shares his feelings and emotions. (If the man you love does this, even once in a while, be sure to praise him. This will encourage more of the same.)
- He is a good athlete or does well at a sport, recreation, or hobby.

・ ・ ・

Now I'll bet more than a few of you feel your hackles rising at the idea of complimenting a man who falls far short of where you'd like him to be. I realize this is the case, but remember, this book is about understanding your husband. If you want him to be more like the man of your dreams, you must nurture and tend to his positive growth—even the very smallest amount of positive growth.

Picture a sapling struggling to make its way out of the soil. It won't become a young tree without lots of watering and fertilizing and pruning. The sapling needs daily care in order to grow, and the same is true with the man in your life.

Does this fit with today's self-focused culture? Definitely not. But it is scriptural. Jesus told his disciples time and again to love and serve one another. The apostle Paul's letters encourage us to build each other up and consider others better than ourselves. In the case of a domineering, victory-driven man, this means that you should search for his winning qualities and praise him. As you do this, you will see that the benefits are amazing. Take a look at the following list:

Benefits of complimenting your husband
- He will feel more kindly toward you.
- He will develop a deep appreciation for you.

- He will see you as his ally and friend.
- He will open up more emotionally.
- He will double his efforts on the thing that you compliment. (For example, if at the appropriate time you say, "Honey, you're such a good listener . . . ," he will feel built up in that area and become determined to continue winning in that area.)
- He will be much more likely to compliment you or view you favorably.
- He will be much less likely to need the affirmation of a stranger or to be tempted into an affair, since you will make him feel like a winner.

There's probably nothing more motivating to me than feeling like I'm satisfying my wife. People can give me standing ovations when I'm speaking or line up across an auditorium to buy my books, but it doesn't mean anything compared to my wife's approval.

I've talked to many successful men and asked them these questions: "How important is your wife's approval and acceptance of you? How important is it that she makes you feel like a winner?"

The responses have been amazing.

Every one of those men said he'd rather have his wife's approval than that of anyone else. Sincere approval from his wife makes a man feel like a winner and keeps him very happy in that relationship.

Making the effort to compliment your husband and focus on the positives doesn't just benefit your husband; it benefits you, too. When you center on the negatives, soon they become so magnified in your mind that they're all you can see. But when you consciously rehearse your spouse's good qualities, you'll be reminded of why you married him. You may find yourself becoming less critical, more grateful, and more loving.

> **What praiseworthy character qualities does your husband have? Where is he ahead of the pack with his decisions, his work habits, his fathering skills, his ability as a husband?**

Here's one thing to remember: Be careful whom you compliment and affirm. Many affairs begin because of the well-meaning praise of a woman. Keep your praise focused on your husband. Find ways to see him as a winner, even if the list of things he does wrong is longer than the list of things he does right. Then keep your attention on his winning traits. Believe me, when you give him your approval and build him up, that's the best motivation for him to develop into the true winner you want him to be.

DAILY LIFE: CAN'T WE GET ALONG?

On an everyday level, the differences in the way men and women go about life might be driving you mad. Let's take a look at a few ways in which testosterone might be causing daily behaviors that are perfectly normal for many men but that you find deplorable.

CLEANLINESS: NEXT TO GODLINESS OR NEXT TO IMPOSSIBLE?

Most men fall short of a woman's expectations in the areas of housework and cleanliness. Sometimes this problem is merely an irritating reminder of everything else that bugs you about the man you love. Other times I've seen it cause outright marriage problems, some strong enough to lead the couple to consider divorce.

Here are a few of the common complaints I hear from women regarding their husbands' housework habits:

- "He mixes colors when he does laundry."
- "He doesn't really clean a bathroom."
- "His idea of a clean kitchen does not involve countertops, stovetops, pots, pans, or the floor."
- "Even when he offers to help, he does every task halfheartedly. I have to go back and do most of it over again."

By the way, one thing most women say in support of their husband is that he does a tremendous job on the yard and other stereotypically male jobs. Here's a list of the chores he may excel at:

- Mowing the lawn
- Keeping up the yard
- Home-improvement tasks or repairs
- Garbage upkeep
- Maintaining the vehicles

The reason men generally seem to be better at these tasks is perhaps because there isn't such scrutiny on the tiny details. No one goes outside and studies whether every single leaf has been swept up. The only noticeable difference after raking leaves is that the leaves are gone. Task accomplished. Leaves conquered.

Housework, however, seems very strange to some men. Bob, a man I met at one of my seminars, related this story to me:

Bob fit very nicely into the generalizations we've been talking about. He liked factual statements and situations and at first resisted helping his wife, Betty, with housework.

CLEANING AND HUSBANDS CAN MIX

Feeling frustrated at your husband's ability to overlook three inches of dust, potato chip crumbs in between the couch cushions, and newspaper strewn all over the floor? Here are a few things to consider:

- **Be realistic.** Maybe your husband is right: Having an immaculate house is not the highest priority. If your high expectations are causing stress in your family, take an honest look and be willing to let go of them.
- **Make a plan.** Sit down with your husband and find a division of responsibilities you can agree on. It doesn't have to be set in stone—you may decide to switch unfavorable chores once a week or once a month.
- **Don't keep score.** Trying to keep your household-chore division completely equitable all the time will drain your energy and will only lead to squabbles and resentment. Plus a constant focus on what's *fair* can make you too concerned with what your spouse owes you—instead of being concerned with how you can serve each other.

"I didn't know what to do," he explained to me.

But in an effort to truly honor his wife, Bob chose to become a new man. Almost overnight he became willing to help Betty around the house. The problem, from his perspective, was that she was rarely satisfied. This became particularly evident once when Betty asked him to clean the downstairs bathroom.

"Sure, honey," Bob told her. "Where's the stuff to clean it with?"

Betty rolled her eyes. "We've lived here two years, and you don't know where the cleaning supplies are?"

Bob felt like a kindergartener flunking his ABCs. He waited until she revealed the hiding spot and then, armed with a bucket full of sponges, wipers, sprays, gels, and powders, he entered the bathroom.

What he saw was a complete surprise.

The bathroom was already clean. Bob looked around to make sure he was right. There was no dirt in the sink, none in the toilet, and none on the floors. He shook his head in confusion, returned the cleaning supplies to the laundry-room hiding place, and then reported back to Betty.

"It's clean," he said. Then he smiled for good measure.

"What?" Betty's eyebrows knitted into two tensely crooked lines. "That's impossible."

She led the way as the two of them returned to the

bathroom. The moment Betty walked through the door she took a single glance around the room and put her hands on her hips. "What do you mean, 'It's clean'?" She grimaced at the sink. "It's filthy."

Bob followed Betty's gaze and squinted. For the life of him, he couldn't see any dirt whatsoever. To hear Betty he'd have expected to see whole colonies of mold and germs the size of house pets.

Since then, Bob told me, he's learned how to clean a bathroom regardless of what he sees. He simply attacks the room as though it did have germs the size of house pets, and even though he sees no difference in the before and after picture, Betty is simply thrilled.

> The reason men generally seem to be better at these [outdoor] tasks is perhaps because there isn't such scrutiny on the tiny details.

So you see, part of the problem is that most men are not detail-oriented when it comes to cleaning. They want the job description and the proper tools, then they want to attack it and get it done. Fast. And as long as a job *looks* done, in their minds it *is* done. That's why cutting the grass is so satisfying. A man might miss a hundred blades of grass or more, but still, the job looks done.

Interestingly, in a much smaller percentage of men, testosterone can work the other way. Instead of being content with a mediocre level of housework, some men feel the house should be perfectly kept. These are the men who get bothered when something is out of place or when the floors don't look clean enough to eat off of. They may have such a need for order—and conquering dirt—that they overlook more important things such as relationships.

A place for everything?

Since we're talking about generalities, let's take a look at the other side of the housework issue: tidiness. Here are some of the things women have said about a man's ability (or lack thereof) to have acceptable household habits:

- "He leaves the toilet seat up even though I've asked him to keep it down."
- "He leaves his clothing all over the house, even though I've asked him to keep it in the hamper."
- "He leaves his dirty dishes at the table or in the sink, even though the dishwasher is empty."
- "He doesn't rinse the sink after brushing his teeth."
- "He empties his pockets wherever he happens to be standing and leaves business cards, bits of trash, and coins all over the house."
- "He doesn't put the next roll of toilet paper on the holder when we run out."

. . .

Now, I realize these issues are important. Very important. But let's consider what men may be thinking as they forget to clean up:

- (As he leaves the toilet seat up) *Now where was that instruction manual? That dishwasher has been making the strangest sound, and no appliance of mine is going to run at half speed. . . .*
- (As he takes off his socks and drops them in various spots around the house) *Okay, if Ben does the presentation at ten tomorrow morning, that'll leave me exactly an hour to convince the VonBrazen company to sign on as part of the deal before someone else decides to. . . .*
- (As he leaves dirty dishes at the table or sink) *If I get the dog leash right now and take him for a run, I can get my exercise in for the day and still be home before the kids fall asleep.*
- (After spitting in the sink) *I have to be up at 5:30 in the morning, so that means I'm down to six hours and twenty-five minutes of sleep if I get to sleep in the next fifteen minutes, but then if I . . .*
- (As he empties his pockets on the freshly scrubbed stovetop) *That solves that problem. I hate having change jingling in my pocket.*
- (As he walks out of the bathroom, leaving the

. . .

toilet-paper holder empty) *I had no idea the Rams acquired that skinny kid as a backup quarterback.* (As he plants himself down on the sofa and tosses the bathroom magazine on the floor) *I'll have to watch the highlights and see if they talk about him. I know one thing for sure, a kid like that isn't what our team needs to win.*

A woman, on the other hand, will be thinking altogether different things in those same situations:

- (As she leaves the bathroom, straightening the wall hanging and adjusting the guest towels) *Even though it's dirty, it'll pass if guests should drop in.*
- (As she takes off her socks and puts them in the hamper) *I'll go ahead and start a load of laundry. That way I'll be ahead of the laundry game come tomorrow.*
- (After brushing her teeth) *That toothpaste spit is so disgusting! I can't imagine anyone leaving that in a sink and walking away.*
- (As she realizes her purse needs cleaning, but continues on without cleaning it) *I hope I find time later today to go through everything here. These coins are so heavy!*
- (As she gets a roll of toilet paper from under the

sink) *I wonder how many rolls are left in the other bathrooms. I should probably put toilet paper on the list so I don't forget to buy some this week at the store.*

If you or your man fits into the categories above, take heart. The suggestions ahead will help you help him develop better habits. But first let's look at two other areas of daily life where the differences between you and the man you love may be blatantly obvious.

DIFFERENCES IN DRIVING

You can really tell the difference in how our brains function when it comes to driving, especially driving at night. Studies show that when couples travel together, the man is behind the wheel 97 percent of the time. Although there are exceptions, men's brains generally are better at determining distances—whether something is thirty feet away or a hundred feet away.

Have you ever been traveling with your husband and been afraid he's going to hit something? Presuming he's truly a safe driver, the reason you feel that way is because what looks dangerous and like not enough room to maneuver a lane change, say, is actually plenty of space by a man's viewpoint.

My personal road victories

The determination to win that we talked about in the last chapter carries over into daily life as well—especially when it comes to driving. My wife and I discovered my own overzealous desire to win when we were driving on vacation. We still laugh at the times when we took off on a vacation and I'd want to get the map out and strategize. I'd want to go about five hundred miles a day and basically make time. My wife had other plans. Sightseeing plans and cute little shop plans.

But even now, when I have a destination in mind, I want to win. The solution is getting to that destination as quickly as possible. I want to get in the car, take off, and get to my destination. The whole time, I'm hoping that nothing distracts me.

> **A gentle answer turns away wrath, but harsh words stir up anger.**
>
> PROVERBS 15:1

On trips we took when our children were younger, I hated to pull over for any reason. When my wife or kids would have to go to the bathroom, it was really tough for me to pull off the freeway into one of those fast-food restaurants for lunch. I wanted them to pack a lunch so we could keep hauling.

If we had to stop for gas, I could understand my wife and kids jumping out to use the restroom. But the whole time I'd be watching the freeway, seeing cars I'd passed miles ago whiz past. I'd mutter something under my breath about why couldn't my family hurry up.

It's only been in recent years that I realized something: It doesn't make me the winner to get there fast. It makes me a tyrant. And that's hard for any woman to live with.

THE TROUBLE WITH WHAT'S ON TV

This will not be a news flash, but men are notorious TV-remote addicts. They can watch upwards of five or six programs at once by flipping channels with the remote and have a general sense of what's happening in every one of them. Women feel practically nauseated having so many channels and programs coming into the room at one time. They spend one minute watching a western in which a woman is about to be abducted by a horse thief, and almost instantly the woman is emotionally involved. *Who is the woman, anyway? Is she someone's girlfriend or wife? Does she have children? And why does the robber want her? Is he in love with her?*

The man is thinking, *Okay, if I turn the channel now I can get back to this in five minutes and find out if the woman lived or not.*

Feelings and facts. It's the same issue we've been

talking about throughout the book. Here are some of the problems that can arise when a couple's television-viewing habits are as different as the couple's described above.

- The woman may feel as though her wishes aren't being considered.
- She may feel as though the man is teasing her with bits of one show after another.
- He may feel that she's nagging him by asking him to stay on a certain channel.
- The woman may walk away, leaving the man to flip through channels alone.

Allowing television constantly to separate you into private worlds in the evening is dangerous to any relationship, especially marriage.

In a nutshell, most women are looking for relational-type programs, whether it's the *Oprah* show or a Hallmark movie-of-the-week. Most men, however, are looking for information: who won the game, who scored the goal, who rescued the woman in the western.

Now that you see how daily life presents issues that can divide and separate you from the man you love, let's take a look at some ways to work around the problem.

LIFE SUPPORT: DON'T TRY TO CONTROL HIM

A man will respond positively to compliments, acceptance, and approval. He will respond negatively to nagging, controlling, and manipulating. As you read through these suggestions for things you can do immediately to change your situation for the better, keep in mind that tone of voice means everything. If you say the right words in a complaining or sarcastic tone, the benefit is lost. So stay positive!

Tools you can use

For housecleaning

- Avoid controlling or manipulating him by looking over his shoulder.
- Avoid calling names, making derogatory comments, or complaining about his housework skills or cleanliness habits.
- Ask him questions about how he thinks the house looks or how he would like it to look. Come up with a plan together to keep it that way.
- In a gentle but forthright way, explain how important it is to you that he clean up after himself.
- Make lists that describe what a certain household task involves, but don't flash them in his face. Simply make them available.
- Sometimes the best and wisest move is simply to pull the toilet seat down and not say another word.

· · ·

For driving

- When your husband is driving, try to keep warnings, gasps, and cautions to a minimum. He will respond better to the occasional needed warning if he doesn't feel like you're evaluating his driving.
- When taking an extended vacation, talk about the trip before you ever get in the car. Let him know you'd like to stop three times (or a specific number of times) so that you can accomplish something (lunch, stretching, sightseeing, etc.).

For television

- Determine what type of television programs interest both of you and watch those together.
- Decide together how many hours a week of television are acceptable, keeping in mind that when one person watches TV alone, his or her spouse may feel isolated.

HEALTHY HABITS: WORK WITH HIM, NOT AGAINST HIM

One of the best examples of spouses working with each other comes from a couple I counseled who struggled over television issues. Scott wanted to spend Sunday afternoons watching football, but his wife, Jenny, hated the background noise, in part because she knew nothing about the game and had no interest in learning.

Compromise came in a very creative way, one that I'd encourage you to try in your situation. This can be especially effective if the love and hate of sports—or any other type of television program—is an issue in your relationship.

This is what they did: Through counseling Scott learned that Jenny would be interested in almost anything that involved relationship. Suddenly a thought occurred to him: *Sports Illustrated* constantly carried articles about the personal and emotional lives of famous athletes.

> **A man will respond positively to compliments, acceptance, and approval. He will respond negatively to nagging, controlling, and manipulating.**

That week he read the magazine more closely than ever before. When the weekend came, he called Jenny in from the computer room and asked her to sit down. Then he pointed at the screen. "You see Number 24?" he said. "That's the quarterback. Next week he's getting married, and his fiancée is scared to death he'll get killed in a game one of these days. He's already had four concussions, and this is the hardest, biggest game of the season. Even his father said he was worried about the game, and his father was his coach when he was just a little boy."

Jenny's expression softened. "His father's at the game?"

Scott leaned further back into the sofa and nodded. "Not just that, but his father is dying of cancer. Even though it's always been his heart's desire to see his son win a championship, and even though this may be his son's last chance, he's more worried about his son's health than the game."

Jenny's eyes welled up with tears. "Can I watch the game with you? Maybe they'll show his dad or his fiancée."

> *Instead, be kind to each other, tenderhearted, forgiving one another, just as God through Christ has forgiven you.*
>
> EPHESIANS 4:32

Imagine this scene in reverse, and you'll understand what I'm asking you to do. If sports are your husband's main interest, find a way to involve yourself. Read sports magazines and look for the feature stories. Almost every player has a story, a secret love, or a reason why the upcoming game is actually very emotional indeed.

I encourage you to take the time to connect with your husband. Far too many affairs start because someone else is willing to be your man's friend, to involve herself in his interests and overlook his annoying habits. But that doesn't have to happen. Find a way to appreciate his favorite activities and get involved. Be his companion. The benefits for your relationship are great.

. . . 6 . . .

UNDERSTANDING IS THE KEY

Throughout this book I've outlined issues and followed them up with Life Support for immediate help and Healthy Habits for the future. We've looked at differences in how men and women talk, how they define intimacy, how they approach recreation, and their habits at home. But the truth is, nothing is more important to the relationship you have with the man you love than simply understanding him.

Know that his brain is soaked in testosterone, grasp the idea that he desires to speak less than you do, and acknowledge that he does not hate you or care less for you because he leaves the toilet seat up. These bits of knowledge will, I pray, go a long way to helping you know, at the very least, that you are not alone.

From this point it's up to you. The more you're willing to work within the parameters that make up the personalities of most men—rather than fighting them or trying to change them—the better your relationship will be. Ignore this crucial information, and you'll find yourself stuck just like before.

> The more you're willing to work within the parameters that make up the personalities of most men—rather than fighting them or trying to change them—the better your relationship will be.

Take this information back to your relationship with your husband and apply the suggestions I've given you. Then stand back and watch how things improve between the two of you.

But do me a favor.

Don't tell him I told you.

BOOKS

Understanding Men

A Choice of Heroes by Mark Gerzon

The Seasons of a Man's Life by Daniel J. Levinson

Ten Stupid Things Men Do to Mess Up Their Lives by Dr. Laura Schlessinger

What Husbands Wish Their Wives Knew about Men by Patrick Morley

Why Men Are the Way They Are by Warren Farrell, Ph.D.

Books for Men

Do Yourself a Favor: Love Your Wife by Page H. Williams

King, Warrior, Magician, Lover by Robert Moore and Douglas Gillette

Man Enough by Frank Pittman, M.D.

Man to Man by Charles R. Swindoll

Raising a Modern-Day Knight by Robert Lewis

Real Men Have Feelings Too by Gary Oliver, Ph.D.

Silent Sons: A Book for and about Men by Dr. Robert J. Ackerman

Differences between Men and Women

Brain Sex—The Real Difference between Men and Women by Anne Moir, Ph.D. and David Jessel

Men Are Clams, Women Are Crowbars by David Clarke, Ph.D.

Passive Men, Wild Women by Pierre Mornell, M.D.

Why Women and Men Don't Get Along! by Carol L. Rhodes, Ph.D. and Norman S. Goldner, Ph.D.

The World according to He and She by Julie Logan and Arthur Howard

Marriage

101 Things Husbands Do to Annoy Their Wives by Ray Comfort

The Art of Loving by Erich Fromm

How to Live with Them Since You Can't Live without Them by Becky and Roger Tirabassi

Reconcilable Differences: Healing for Troubled Marriages by Jim Talley

Sexuality or the Body

The Male Body by Abraham Morgentaler, M.D.

The New Male Sexuality by Bernie Zilbergeld, Ph.D.

Sex and the Brain by Jo Durden-Smith and Diane deSimone

Sex on the Brain by Deborah Blum

Issues

The Angry Man by David Stoop, Ph.D. and Stephen Arterburn

Freeing Someone You Love from Alcohol and Other Drugs by Ronald L. Rogers and Chandler Scott McMillin

When Men Batter Women by Neil Jacobson, Ph.D. and John Gottman, Ph.D.

If Men Are Like Buses Then How Do I Catch One? by Michelle McKinney Hammond

A Time to Dance by Karen Kingsbury

AUDIOCASSETTES

Spiritual Renewal in Counseling by Stephen Arterburn

WEB SITES

Family Research Council—www.frc.org

Focus on the Family—www.family.org

Heritage Foundation—www.heritage.org

National Marriage Project—http://marriage.rutgers.edu

RADIO PROGRAMMING

Family Life Today—Dennis Rainey and Bob Lepine; www.familylife.com

Focus on the Family—Dr. James Dobson; www.family.org

New Life Live—Dr. Paul Meier, Henry Cloud, Stephen Arterburn

CONFERENCES AND SEMINARS

FamilyLife Marriage Conferences; www.familylife.com

"I Still Do" Arena Events; www.familylife.com

FREE! Downloadable discussion guide

for this and other Tyndale titles at

 ChristianBookGuides.com

1 Anne Moir, Ph.D., and David Jessel, *Brain Sex: The Real Difference between Men and Women* (New York: Dell Publishing, 1989), 75.

2 *Brain Sex,* rev. ed. (New York: Carol Publishing Group, 1991), 82.

3 Ibid., 79-80.

4 Robert Kohn, "Patterns of Hemispheric Specialization in Pre-Schoolers," *Neurophychologia* 12: 505–512.

5 Dave Barry, *Dave Barry's Complete Guide to Guys: A Fairly Short Book* (New York: Random House, 1995), 65.

6 John Gray, *Men Are from Mars, Women Are from Venus* (New York: HarperCollins, 1992), 18–19.

7 Ibid., 31.

8 Dean Ornish, *Love and Survival: The Scientific Basis for the Healing Power of Intimacy* (Thorndike, Maine: Thorndike Press, 1998), 14.

Marriage Alive International, Inc., founded by husband-wife team Claudia and David Arp, MSW, is a nonprofit marriage- and family-enrichment ministry dedicated to providing resources, seminars, and training to empower churches to help build better marriages and families. The Arps are marriage and family educators, popular speakers, award-winning authors, and frequent contributors to print and broadcast media. They have appeared as marriage experts on programs such as *Today, CBS This Morning,* and *Focus on the Family.* Their Marriage Alive seminar is in great demand across the U.S. and in Europe.

The Mission of Marriage Alive is to identify, train, and empower leaders who invest in others by building strong marriage and family relationships through the integration of biblical truth, contemporary research, practical application, and fun.

Our Resources and Services

- Marriage and family books and small-group resources
- Video-based educational programs including *10 Great Dates to Energize Your Marriage* and *Second Half of Marriage*
- Marriage, pre-marriage, and parenting seminars, including *Before You Say "I Do," Marriage Alive, Second Half of Marriage,* and *Empty Nesting*
- Coaching, mentoring, consulting, training, and leadership development

CONTACT MARRIAGE ALIVE INTERNATIONAL AT
WWW.MARRIAGEALIVE.COM OR (888) 690-6667.

The Smalley Relationship Center, founded by Dr. Gary Smalley, offers many varied resources to help people strengthen their marriage and family relationships. The Center provides marriage enrichment products, conferences, training material, articles, and clinical services—all designed to make your most important relationships *successful* relationships.

The Mission of the Smalley Relationship Center is to increase marriage satisfaction and lower the divorce rate by providing a deeper level of care. We want to help couples build strong, successful, and satisfying marriages.

Resources and Services:

- Nationwide conferences: Love Is a Decision, Marriage for a Lifetime
- Counseling services: Couples Intensive program, phone counseling
- Video series, including *Keys to Loving Relationships, Homes of Honor,* and *Secrets to Lasting Love*
- Small group leadership guide
- Articles on marriage, parenting, and stepfamilies
- Smalley Counseling Center provides counseling, national intensives, and more for couples in crisis

CONTACT SMALLEY RELATIONSHIP CENTER AT WWW.SMALLEYONLINE.COM OR 1-800-84-TODAY.